KNIFE CRIM

By Adil The Author

Author: Adil The Author

Book cover credit: Adil The Author

DISCLAIMER

This book does not in any way or form advise or influence anyone to commit crime but rather raise awareness and encourage others there is many ways to prevent a life of violence.

Some context of this book is possibly fabricated for the mere understanding of the reader; however most of this book is based on real life experience, which is true and factual. The contents within this book is influenced by the authors own views and experience. No responsibility is taken for any action implicated.

Some paragraphs or content may offend the reader or be too raw for the reader to handle, therefore if you are easily offended please find another book to read.

CONTENTS

"The more that you read,

the more things you know,

the more that you learn,

the more places you'll go"

- Dr Seuss

ACKNOWLEDGEMENT

First and foremost, praise be to god, whom with that nothing is possible.

I bear witness that there is no god but Allah and Muhammad is the Messenger of Allah and that Islam is the truth and the only way to live your life, if you seek to fulfil true contentment or purpose in your life wanting to understand the reason of your existence. I do not believe we was created in vanity, but to strive and fulfil the commandments of God. I also believe in all previous monotheist religions and hope god guides you to the truth.

DEDICATION

This book is dedicated in loving memory of Joshua White aka Abdul Aziz who tragically lost his life to knife crime in Hackney, East London on Friday 26th April 2019, as a result of being stabbed in the heart just shortly after leaving the masjid (mosque) for Friday prayers. You will never be forgetting and I pray for you daily.

May Allah (God) have mercy on your soul. Ameen (Amen).

FOREWORD

This self-help book exploits the subject of violence which roots from anger and offers short solutions with concise pragmatic practical help. I am a prisoner serving a custodial sentence for a violent offence. I full well know how hard it can be to repress anger. Therefore, throughout the course of this book I will deconstruct the prevalent subject.

Violence is a result of a mental disease 'Anger'. This is the core of this which will be educated for anyone whom suffers from anger problems and actually lashes out with fierce violence.

"Even if I can save one person from the doomed pit anger, I would consider my mission successful and this self-help book worth writing, from within in a prison cell" - Adil The Author

INTRODUCTION

The idea of this book was originated in a prison cell named HMP Onley. Just me and my thoughts in silence, incarcerated for violence. I have spent nearly up to a decade behind prison walls and along my journey I have met various difference people from diverse backgrounds, all different types of cultures and races. You will never witness so many men co-existing in one place by force, except in prison. It is a strange but surreal and unique experience on an individual basis.

I am serving a lengthy custodial sentence and as a prisoner have travelled throughout the HMP system from category prisons, B cat, C cat and even D cat. My violent offence I was convicted of was for section 18 GBH aged just 23. At such a young age; we often think that we know it all but the truth is we know very little about life and have very little figured out.

Prison gave me the unwanted time to reflect on my actions and how I ended up in a harsh predicament of serving a lengthy sentence. To the public eye -prison is all about the government's favourite word 'rehabilitation' but the truth is very little rehabilitation takes place in prison. How can you rehabilitate a human by locking them up and keeping them caged? As humans we are not built for such living circumstances.

Yet there are thousands of prisoners up and down the UK in prisons who are serving sentences and upon release are likely to come back to prison. NOMS (National offender management system) revealed that three out four prisoners are likely to be re-called within the first year of being released. This statistic itself is evidence that rehabilitation in prison is scarce, but is something within yourself.

Rehabilitation is 'to help someone get back to their normal self.

(According to oxford English dictionary)

So as prisoners we have to reform our self to what is normal in society, what I assume is work and home, also known as the '9 to 5' life. As a prisoner myself I can tell you that there are some real genuine troubled prisoners who are frustrated with some serious mental health problems that need to be addressed.

In prison, very little is done to understand why such a person ended up with such issues, you cannot put a prisoner on one million different psychological courses, just to tick boxes, but the truth is it all looks good on paper to present for the person higher up the echelon within the prison justice system. Yet, all it simply comes down to is hindsight and when the prisoner himself learns 'enough is enough', because hindsight is hindsight it is irreplaceable. Prisoners are intractable, even more so than children or a new born baby. No prisoner wants to be a prisoner or reside in prison; except for those who I have met and openly admit they require shelter which is understandable, but my point is it takes a collective co-operative effort from probation staff, prison 'justice' system and prisoners. Most importantly, prisoners, criminals and the misunderstood youth are both the problem and the solution, so until we all understand this there can be no rehabilitation.

We have to take responsibility and completely understand 'rehabilitation' or 'change' as I like to call it, is solely down to us as individuals. Change can be one of the hardest things in life to process and actually follow through with action; it is hard I get it. Nevertheless no matter what opinion is displayed or argument is presented; it does not get rid of the fact that change starts within you!

TRIGGERS OF VIOLENCE

If you want to question alcoholics, then the most suitable place to find them would be a pub, similarly if you want to find people of violence, then the most common location to find them would be a prison. Being a prisoner myself of a violent crime; I realised the hard way that violence is sad epidemic amongst youth especially with the disease of 'knife crime'.

Whilst in prison I came across many prisoners who were serving sentences for different degrees of violence. Commonly, I would ask "what was the trigger or cause behind your act of violence?" and I received a variety of different purposes such as; I lost the plot; I was pissed off; I don't know what I was thinking; he disrespected me; my pride was damaged; she provoked me; There was an endless list but I realised most of the violent acts rooted from anger. Nevertheless, there were many other causes and factors to their acts of violence but anger was the primary reason. I am not saying their violence is understandable, rather I was merely investigating research for this book you are reading and here is what I found out from prison walls.

<u>Triggers of violence</u>

Anger issues (i.e. strong feeling of displeasure)

Money problem (i.e. I am angry; I'm broke or have debt issues)

Vindictive personality (i.e. revenge and grudges)

Drug-fuelled (i.e. competing in drug dealing)

Postcode wars (i.e. conflict of gang areas)

Pride/Ego (i.e. excessive self-respect)

Envy & Jealousy (i.e. Yearning others life and wishing harm)

Acrimonious events (i.e. bitter over an event)

Mental health (i.e. Paranoia, Schizophrenia)

These are nine of the most common triggers behind why most people commit acts of violence when researched from within prison myself. I will now elucidate each point for better understanding because to avoid violence you must understand the causes in order to dodge such encounters. Otherwise, there could be a chance of you being in a unnecessary predicament or worse.

Anger Issues

Anger often derives from 'a disliked matter', meaning you have a sense of value or a sentimental meaning towards a matter and someone else objects resulting in anger, tension and conflict. Anger is a hot emotion and erases dialectic thoughts, Anger brings nothing good in your life, avoid it all costs.

Money Problems

Money itself is a confusing aspect of life. All the good and bad comments, which surrounded money. A typical statement is 'money is the root of evil' but the truth is money is only what you are -it is a tool of expression allowing you to be kind or evil. Rather it is people that are evil and money which is innocent. It is the greed and lust of people which turn them to do crimes for money. Back to the subject at hand, it is often found that violent crimes do occur for money; weapons being used, families being kidnapped, and people being tortured. No criminals want to be on the receiving end, but how do such people think with a criminal train of thought. Commonly, most criminals admitted to me that they grew up 'broke' and for some weird reason the 'working' lifestyle does not suffice, so the next available job is 'crime'. They are angry they grew up broke and have resent residing within them self and use extreme violence to get rid of the anger and gain money. A mental disease such as: lust, greed, envy, and jealousy that are causing factors. If you have money problems, seek money management courses or read books on it. Being broke is only a symptom, especially if you have the ability to work you should.

People who have a vindictive personality have a strong urge to commit revenge and usually do follow through with action. Such a negative attitude stems from issues from the past because for one to commit an act of revenge it means there had to have been a previous encounter. The first incident is a prerequisite for revenge to actually take place. The common thought of 'I want to get him back' - This is well known to people who hold grudges. In life, we create most of our problems; for men are troublesome, and when trouble troubles you then no human likes it.

I am still waiting to meet a lifer prisoner who does not regret their act of revenge due to a long-held grudge from the past. I have travelled throughout the prison system for ten complete years and have not met a single man who is content with the violent crime they committed. A lifer once made a powerful statement to me, whom I will never forget and it was. 'If violence was the answer to everything, then how many scars would every human on earth have?". Violence causes more problems than it solved.

Drug-fuelled

I have met a common debate in prison amongst prisoners and even prison staff, which is: 'What us worse - drugs or robbery?'. They are both just as bad as each other. The typical argument of but when you sell drugs, you are not hurting anyone - they smoke it by choice'. In essence, what a drug dealer is doing is passing a 'knife' to the addict for them to harm their self by consuming drugs.

When selling drugs, it is relative to violence because guns and drugs go hand in hand. It is an illegal business industry of narcotics and violence. Competition to wipe out your rivals. An ex drug dealer stated "I have met a hell of a lot of serious people but I can tell you I have not met a single man who lives a peaceful life from selling drugs: My point is the drug industry and violence works together leading to unwanted problems. Even more it is dangerous because the past can catch up with you."

Postcode wars

Andrew Pritchard, a man who was dubbed as 'Britain's biggest cocaine smuggler' stated "I really don't understand what they are killing each other over, gang territory, an area or postcode that they probably at such young ages and not even afford to buy a brick in that postcode, never mind a house'. This is harsh but true. For me, it is the saddest trigger of violence for me, because those who indulge in such fields have openly admitted to me in prison: 'The worst thing is the guys I got beef with, we all went to the same school and our families know each other'. So, people must ask themselves, when will it stop? Answer: Never, maybe it is too late. Once you put your hand in the fire, then you have already been burnt. You may be willing to let go. Majority who are stuck in such a war on the streets will gain hindsight when they have wasted their precious life in prison - that is if they are lucky enough not to be in a coffin.

A reformed criminal once said, "Talking and being clever in hindsight sounds brilliant but you have to go through an actual experience to gain the hindsight". In the context of this subject of postcode wars - it means 'they will learn the hard way', if they do not learn from those of the past because history repeats itself. Gang conflict is a one-way road which splits to two roads named 'Jail' or 'Death'. It brings no good and is scary as you may move on and someone you troubled years ago has not, hence it can catch up with you, making it a risky worthless and cheap lifestyle.

Pride/Ego

This trigger is the most ignorant and arrogant act of violence out of the nine triggers, because it can be avoided so easily. The worst scenario I have heard of is a man lost his life simply because he accidently stepped on another man's trainers at a nightclub and as a result was shot. The aggressor had excessive self-respect and stupidly intended to harm or kill an innocent man over such a trivial matter. I seriously cannot comprehend what went through his mind. For people with such a thought process; they must remember it is unjust and it is a better cause of action. 'to treat others how you would like to be treated'. You must learn to crush your ego by stepping on it and WALK AWAY.

Envy and Jealousy

These two traits belong to the foolish person, such people are normally envious and jealous coveting the possessions of someone who they do not even know the background of or the struggle they went through to obtain their belongings, yet for some weird reason are angry and bitter. This mentality breeds envy and jealousy.
It is not understandable at all. There is no reason or excuse for anyone on the face of this earth to act in such a way or even feel a way. How can you be envious wishing harm on someone for doing nothing? It does not make any logical sense. It is stupidity and you just waste your own focus and energy with feelings of malice and hatred. Instead, you could have used your energy to focus and elevate yourself.

Acrimonious events

This type of self-inflicted anger is widespread within prisons for many criminals are angry and bitter at being confined within a prison cell. Boxing legend, Floyd Mayweather served a few months in prison for a violent offence and he admitted in an interview for HBO, stating: "Prison does drive you mad, Being locked up does make you angry and you will have this anger built up inside you and nowhere to vent it". I have served nine complete years and counting. In fact, I am even over tariff, whereas Floyd Mayweather only served a few months. This made him realise how one becomes frustrated and gradually builds up anger. Even up until today I still get angry which is sane and normal but I know as long as I do not act upon that anger, then I am allowed to get as angry as I want. Every human has a capacity of anger, which is a natural emotion but the wise and appropriate person does not act upon it, because they have either learnt or know how venomous it can be and bring a toxic outcome.

Mental/psychological problems

I am no doctor or psychologist but it can be easily detected when someone behaves out of the norm and has mental problems. There are people like this but they are rarely seen in prison because they get sectioned as they suffer from illnesses such as paranoia and schizophrenia etc.

IDENTIFY YOURSELF

Identifying yourself is you addressing your anger issues.

Identifying yourself is understanding why you are angry

Identifying yourself is making you aware of the root of your anger

Identifying yourself is knowing what triggers your angry response

Identifying yourself is comprehending the provocations of anger.

This chapter is all about you identifying yourself through assessment of self-analysis. Violence stems from anger, so to reduce and get rid of violence we must uproot it from its secure which is anger. It is an emotion no human can avoid no matter how hard they try but what we can do as humans is control ourselves.

To maintain or control anything we must understand how it functions and give its due cure. There is a chapter name 'cure violence with silence', but this aspect will be further explained in the book. As of now, we will look at what makes one angry and this is exactly what I mean by identifying yourself.

In the previous chapter 'Triggers of violence', I listed nine primary causes of violence. This was for the reader to analyse and highlight exactly which category they may fall under. (Refer back to 'triggers of violence' on page 13, to read these triggers)

All nine triggers are relative to anger in one way or another. It is for this reason I focus on tackling the issue of anger through self-analytical questions such as:

Why do I get angry?

How do I feel after releasing my anger through violence?

How do I feel when I am angry?

What can I do to address my anger?
How long have I had this anger within me?
Is my anger self-inflicted?

Such questions give you more of an understanding of yourself. It raises self-awareness of the problem. This is vital because if you are not aware of an issue, then how can you provide a situation.

Having no awareness will allow the problem to go undetected and flow back and forth in your life repeatedly. Hence, you must be self-analytical regarding your anger and appropriately wean the problem.

I went through the same process but first I had to understand and study the problem being discussed, which was 'What is violence?'

WHAT IS VIOLENCE?

Violence: *'Actions using physical force intended to harm or kill'*

(Oxford English dictionary 2011)

All my crimes committed have been orientated with violence and
I was incarcerated for my violent actions. Prison gives you plenty of unwanted time to reflect on self-analytical questions regarding my detrimental behaviour. Questions directed at myself, such as:

How do I feel when I commit violence?

Did I really intend to harm the person with violence?

Do my actions affect just me or the victim of violence?

How can I stop my acts of violence?

Why or what is the cause of my violence?

The last question (Why or what is the cause of my violence) is the most vital to my rectification, because a problem not investigated is a problem waiting to happen again especially a problem that is not eradicated.
It was not long after I came to the short thesis that violence is a result of anger. Having thought of it continually in my prison cell, I don't know what it is about violence, but it seems as if it has an attraction. Look at the sports of boxing and cage fighting - they are prime examples of violent attractions.

It is a fact that people do find violence amusing and many are under a false pretence of admitting so. Violence us not acceptable in society and those who break the laws are often sentenced to prison, and then gain hindsight after a tough experience. My point is a dialectic approach to violence saves the process of living and learning through an unpleasant situation like prison.

Here is something to consider, if there was an award show and the award went to "THE MOST STUPID THING EVER", then violence would be the only nominee and winner, because there is nothing more stupid than it.

Anger is a seed and violence is the bitter fruit produced. Along came the most important question of my life, 'what makes you angry?'. This question popped up, after struggling to admit to myself that I do have anger issues which I have to address. This allowed me to identify myself for rectification, being a lifer prisoner, you have a lot of time to think and sort your head out but I can tell you learning from the words of another man is better than going through a violent experience with violence.

MY EXPERIENCE WITH VIOLENCE

My experience with violence has been bitter and bought nothing but negativity into my life plus years and years in prison. No human likes being locked up, but being caged can turn you animalistic. World boxing championship, Floyd Mayweather served a short prison sentence and upon release admitted, "Being locked up breed's self-inflicted anger".

Anger is nothing but a strong feeling of displeasure and if it goes undetected it can have catastrophic consequences. My 'trigger of violence' was my 'pride and ego'. Through years of reflection and rumination. I gained hindsight as well as learning to crush my pride by stepping on it which allowed me to humble myself through religion and experience. Ego is not a bad thing but excessive ego can be, and I had to re-shape my own sense of value in regards to my life to eradicate anger plus violence.
Violence and anger are bad relatives to humans. If I was to write a letter to the pair, it would be something like this.

"Dear violence and anger,
I hate you both so much and I am upset with you for the no good you deceptively have bought me, because at the time of anger - it makes perfect sense to commit violence for you are a strong emotion which over rides any other feeling.

You are deceptive because in a temporary state of anger - you persuade me to commit violence and at the time it makes total sense but afterwards when you leave, all I feel is regret and sorrow because of the consequences.

I am departing from you on this day onward, so please just leave me alone. Goodbye, anger and just to let you know if you ever try come into my life - I will ignore you due to your ugliness. As for violence you are just as deceptive and bad. I have departed from anger, so there is no need for you to stay in touch. You are like suicide, Yes, you violence! You are exactly like suicide in the sense that you only bring harm to one's self and frequent death.

If violence was a male, I would hate him, if violence was a female, I would hate her. Violence is akin to suicide. It paves a pathway for you to possibly get killed. You may be willing to let past matters go but others who are vindictive may not, making violence become a vicious cycle. You only hurt yourself when you hug and welcome violence in your life. The person in front of you, yourself and everyone you love is hurt.

The offender who uses violence ends up in prison, the victims of violence end up in a grave and both families are both innocent bystanders and this is often the case.

Violence is a gun which is aimed at your own head. It is a crazy vicious cycle which goes around and around until you or the person in front of you is dead. So, you may as well throw the first punch at yourself if you are thinking it is a pragmatic solution to your problem, then you thought wrong.

You hurt yourself, your family and those 'enemies' of yours who stand in front of you. You affect those who are not involved and are wrong. Therefore, this is where me and you go our separate ways. Goodbye."

This letter to violence and anger was written in a court cell almost immediately after I was sentenced, but I have added a few words due to recent experience. It is only after breathing years of prison I realised I am walking evidence of the proven conclusion that you can 'cure violence with silence'.

CURE VIOLENCE WITH SILENCE

Violence is a negative force in life, whereas silence is a positive facility in life. In a world that has a mixture of culture and races. Life's diversity when presents to anyone can be arduous to co-exist and get along with other with polarization amongst everyone in this new dawn of social media easily expressing opinions. Humans are selfish creatures for we only race to seek that which benefits us first. The presence of male and female results in domestic violence sometimes. Why? Every human is argumentative one way or another it just depends on the subject with opposing views.

One is hot, and the other is cool. Violence is hot, silence is to be cool. The solution to violence is the process of transmitting a negative into a positive. It is to channel that negative energy to produce a positive outcome. Curing violence with silence you have to treat the problem with the opposing force. They are of moderation and counter-balance. One or the other meaning day and night, hot and cold, heaven and hell, husband and wife. There is an endless list which I can mention but I would not want you reading a 200-page book. When the matter in hand can be elucidated in a concise manner.

Violence is never the answer - it causes more problems than it solves, if you look at the mass scale of war around the world, specifically the Middle East. America and UK government have shot themselves in the foot. They have thrown stones elsewhere whilst living in a glass house. They have verbally abused other whilst possessing a glass jaw. In other words, they have bought the war in the Middle East back on to the streets of Britain through their own acts of violence. My point is violence only begets violence. Even the most fragile of people in society; If they are bullied or have their back pushed against the wall they will react and the reaction will not be a pleasant one at all the aggressor or bully.

I have witnessed this first-hand in prison and been on both sides - the receiving and the giving end. It only leads to disaster. Violence is a result of the detrimental emotion 'Anger': Every single human in life possesses three different faculties, which coexist within and they are:

Anger

Desire

Intellect

Whatever mental capacity is the strongest at any given time will automatically over-ride the other two and that is a fact. To control yourself from committing violence - you have to audit your anger, meaning 'you must sort your head out' as anger is a mental state. Again, the process of you having to identify yourself and treating it with silence.

BENEFITS OF SILENCE

Silence pregnates priority

Silence breeds rumination

Silence allows you to reflect

Silence exercise patience

Silence is a form of solace

Silence is meditation

Silence promotes relaxation

Silence is a prerequisite for brilliant ideas

Silence stimulates the brain

Silence leads to rectitude

Silence paves a way to a moment of bliss

Silence increases thoughts of clarity in life

Silence allows you to see things for what they are in life with closed eyes

Silence promotes reason

It allows you to relax with no distractions and think long and hard about what really matters, which soon allows you to choose the correct course of action. Silence requires patience, and patience is something no generation has had, especially this generation of youth today. The truth is there is no replacement for silence. In a loud world full of hustle and bustle, one is always occupies not allowing to soak up the benefits of silence. Two places I have realised through experience which are salient for silence are graveyards and prison cells, as I have lost my older brother and my mother at a young age and have served over tariff of my sentence totalling nearly up to a decade behind prison walls. In fact, here is a piece of poetry I wrote in silence whilst in prison:

"Wise people often benefit from silence in isolation
Isolation breeds reflection
Reflection plants a seed for faith
Faith leads to reality
Reality is death
Death who prepares for it - The wise."

The concise poem you just read regarding the reality of life from a religious perspective and how the wise person contemplates life truly is short, therefore prepares for the hereafter (i.e. Heaven or hell) with virtuous deeds. Just like every other piece of test it is open to objection and argumentation, but that is my thought/opinions, which I am rightly entitled to. My point I emphasise is when one is silent - it allows you to ruminate on matters clearly and realise that the 'violent' situation you want to occur is most likely trivial and will be regrettable in the nearby future, but when one is angry it clouds logic/reason except for those who understand the psychology of anger.

PSYCHOLOGY OF ANGER

Psychology is the study of the human mind and its functions. Anger us a strong emotion which resides within every single human but some react to it more than others. Everyone has the capacity of anger but not everyone but not everyone acts upon it but why is this so?

Anger often is the silent emotion with a loud message. In my experience, those who I have met that suffer from anger issues are frequently quiet in prison. Anger itself can be incoherent, but very natural as an emotional or reaction. Anger can make you believe or to actually take action to do something horrid towards a person for an unjust act. Anger no doubt leads to problems; Anger can derive from thoughts that one has been disrespectful, bullied or treated unfairly. Therefore, the chapter IDENTIFYING YOURSELF is very helpful to understand the impetus of your anger.

Anger is a temporary mindset deriving from our thoughts. It can be said: 'anger is but a thought', so if you want to work on your anger then you must work on your mind (i.e. Thought process), when one is angry it stimulates the adrenaline of the body and its response. The main typical two responses that are famously known "fight or flight". A binary thought process of fight or walk away. We will act upon one or the other due to cognition because of the psychology of anger.

Anger can be defined below by three human communications:

Thoughts ›› Feelings ›› Behaviour

Thoughts:	He disrespected me, or it is unfair etc
Feelings:	anger, adrenaline, hot, intense
Behaviour:	urge to fight, attack or shout

Thoughts

Often, we make up scenarios in our head and create our own problems. We make a micro problem into a macro problem. Talk is cheap, words do not hold commodity especially those of others. So, do not take it seriously.

Self-defeating thoughts such as; he disrespected me, he was rude, he took my respect for a joke - all creating negative thoughts. If one hundred people verbally abuse you on one hundred different occasions, then you cannot lash out every time. It is the process of mental growth and maturity to walk away, but it so hard when we have strong anger feelings.

Feelings

If every single human only acted upon negative feelings, then life would be a disaster. Feelings are a temporary mindset and change as frequent as the English weather (i.e. every other minute). Similarly, at the specific moment of anger - we think of war and conflict not peace and serenity. Anger is deceptive because at the time of anger it convinces you that violence is the most reasonable answer as 'violence will make you feel better'. Anger is a hot temper and you need to be cool by ventilation. So, find a process of venting that best suits you. (See chapter Pragmatic Solutions on page 36)

Behaviours

The behavioural symptoms of an angry person are clearly visible and in some extreme cases the one who suffers from anger even looks possessed by a demon or evil spirit. Symptoms include angry facial expression, breathing heavily, huffing and puffing, arguing (yelling and shouting), urge to attack, staying silent by inwardly seething, fist clenching, snapping at others etc. These are the primary symptoms that have been listed.

These three psychological functions, thoughts, behaviour and feeling lead to a body reaction (flight or fight) which is triggered by the body alarm system to engross in fighting or walk away. With us humans we always have two options, and we must pick the correct one without emotions like anger interfering, for anger overrides intellect, logic and sense. Take the fiction character 'The Hulk' as an example, when exposed to his triggers of anger then he turns green and want to smash everything. Whereas, for humans instead of green we often turn red with our face as an expression of anger.

Violence and anger are inter-related being common traits amongst men. The UK prison population estimate consists of 83,000 prisoners in 2019 and 79,000 are believed to be men and the other 4,000 women [accurate as of 2019]. Myself having served nearly a decade around violent criminals and murderers gave me the unwanted privilege to realise a lot of violence acts as well as conflict arises from the ego of men. Many have lost their life and may have been sentenced to life; just because both the aggressor and victim were not willing to let their ego deplete.

EGO DEPLETION MODEL

Ego – 'A person's sense of their own value'

(Oxford English dictionary 2011)

There is a widely spread epidemic about the misconception of one's ego amongst men especially, as well as women but it is a more common issue amongst men. There have been many debates as to discuss whether ego is a good facet or bad aspect of a human's life. In prison I had a lengthy discussion with a psychologist and we collectively concluded ego is fine but in fact it is super-ego that is wrong.

As humans we all demand respect and mutual fair treatment. When someone 'crosses the line' by disrespecting one, then it can manifest or explode into frustration, agitation even anger – the trio leading to violence. What I have learnt in prison about ego and superego. I would like to share with you. Violence amongst men commonly roots from the clash of superego's, especially in prison. I will now explain the slight difference between the two.

Ego vs Superego

Ego is self-value in short and this is strongly shaped through one's upbringing especially what the parents feed to the child's brain as they will grow to adopt this belief. Ego can also be determined by the meaning of value one gives to their own self. Common aspects of one's own sense of value can be respect, honour and morals.

Superego (according to Britannia encyclopaedia 1994-2011).

"One of the three aspects of the human personality along with the ID and ego. The last three elements to develop, the superego is the ethical component of the personality, providing the moral standards by which the ego operates. The superego is

formed during the first five years of life in response to parental punishment and approval; children internalise their parent's moral standards as well as those of the surrounding society and the developing superego serves to control aggressive or other socially unacceptable impulses". Violation of the superegos standards gives rise to feelings of guilt, rage or anxiety.

The above elucidates the terminology of both ego and superego. There is a huge difference but at the same time a very thin line between the pair. In fact. whilst in prison I booked an appointment to see a psychologist named Innocent Okorie and we had a lengthy discussion on the subject at hand. The conclusion of the conversation was 'ego is not a bad thing, but superego is a bad thing'. *(All definitions below are according to Oxford English Dictionary 2011)*

I will now explain a theory named ***'EGO DEPLETION MODEL'*** and exploit the differences between 'ego' and 'superego'.

EGO DEPLETION MODEL

EGO (A person's self-value)

Pride	Honour	Respect
To be proud of one's qualities, achievements or possessions	Great respect and sense of what is morally right	Consideration for the feelings or rights of others

SUPEREGO (A person's self-value)

Conceit	High Self-Esteem
Excessive pride in one's own self above others	Extreme consideration that one is superior and only care's for one's self

As I stated earlier there is a huge difference between ego and superego but simultaneously a very thin line between the pair, and here is why. Superfluous means 'more than required'. In other words, Superfluous is excessiveness or extra. Every human will have a sense of self value and respect for their self because in order for the others to respect you then you must require self-respect. However, superego is ego that is superfluous.

Therefore, develop moderation in ego through the principle of 'treat others how you would like to be treated' because no human prefers disrespect over respect. I conclude by stating 'superego is not your amigo' and I learnt this from living years within the most violent place on earth.

MOST VIOLENT PLACE ON EARTH

Prison is the most violent place on earth. Prison simultaneously houses violent criminals from diverse backgrounds along with their enemies. Prison is a battlefield and a library at the same time - you have to read situations, then act accordingly. I spent years within the HMP system and have quite an experience. HMP Belmarsh where I have spent time is home to some of the UK's most ruthless, dangerous and violent criminals.

Severe acts of violence usually end in two ways - either way you end up in a box, meaning a prison cell or a grave. You either end up losing your life or serving a prison sentence for life. Uncontrolled anger that usually spills into bloody violence leads to isolation and here is why.

Anger not controlled leads you to the urge of committing a violent act, which lands you in prison. So, you are now socially excluded from society within prison which breeds more anger as you are in a continuous regime of being locked up and controlled. This self-inflicted anger builds up and you lash out with violence having prison fights leading to 'BLOCK', which is segregation otherwise known inmate isolation from the normal jail population. Hence uncontrolled anger leads to isolation literally.

I know a friend who in his youth was a very violent criminal and continually lashed out at others. He was such a problem and had to be housed in category AA (double A Cat) prisons due to his violent acts. A prison cell; isolated from the rest of the prisoners including segregation (block) because you are that much of a threat and the only company you have left is your thoughts. The only person left to lash out against is yourself, so will you then punch yourself in the face?

Like I stated earlier, violence is akin to suicide because you are entering a harmful competition with the potential death of you taking place and the candidate are violent criminals competing. Violence is a gun which is aimed at your own head.

Violence is a vicious cycle which goes around and around; until you are dead or the person in front of you. So, you may as well punch yourself in the face because you hurt yourself, your family and these 'enemies' of yours in front of you. The consequences of one act of violence does effect more than two people (i.e. aggressor and victim).

I will never forget the moment when a lifer prisoner serving thirty years for murder, looked me in the eye and calmly said *"Our enemies are our evil thoughts. Our enemies were once our friend and this happens often. Verbal conflict with friends to a limit can be good. It is a process of purification because if you see these 'friends' as good or bad. It allows you to see how much or less that person means to you in the first place and yeah conflict with violence makes you feel better because you have vented but it is a hot emotion which requires cool ventilation, plus at the time hurting someone makes total complete sense but the truth is* ***THERE IS NO BIGGER HURT TO YOURSELF THAN LOSING YOUR FREEDOM."***

In prison violence occurs over the most trivial matters. The ego of different men clashes and results in more problems. Such situations of violence especially in the streets where there are weapons usually have two different episodes of violence.

Episode 1. Two lives preserved, as 1 walk away

Episode 2. One life lost and One sentenced to life

When ego's clash, you must remember, if you want violence to solve the issue remember there will always be someone stronger than you. People of often have the misconception that the physically bigger person is stronger in conflict and this is not true *because 'the weak man holds the balance between his life and the life of the fearless strong man'*. How?

By walking away and retracting himself from the situation - 'The weak man comes out stronger as he has not allowed the strongman to dictate the situation. So, the weak man comes out on top because all he did was THINK and WALKAWAY with his PRAGMATIC SOLUTIONS.

PRAGMATIC SOLUTIONS

This chapter provides sensible, reasonable and effective methods as an answer to the problems of anger issues plus violence. The root must be eradicated, not the branch or leaf. When tackling the epidemic of violence, we must dig deeper and understand it does stem from those who have anger issues with the urge to act in a violent manner. Hence, I address the issue head on - so it prevents potential violence.

Anger is a mental state and emotion. Therefore, we must shift our attention to the non-physical (mind) over the physical (body). Ultimately, when angry you must **THINK** and walk away.

The Hatred Inside Never Keep

Hatred is to strongly disapprove or dislike something and no-one likes being disrespected but when someone experiences disrespect, then it can damage their ego even breeding hatred and they end up harbouring feelings like a grudge. To be honest, in life to get along with every single person is difficult due to varied cultures, persons and backgrounds. So, the best course of action for one to take is to keep them self to them self or mingle appropriately respecting boundaries of others. For this approach reduces major chances of ego's or personalities clashing and preserves dignity plus potential violent conflicts at extreme.

Hatred is a negative emotion and brings nothing good. Hatred should not mix in the mind of a truly good character for this emotion or thought process should be foreign and unfamiliar to them if they are on the true verge of self-improvement.

My point is hatred can breed anger, and at the moment of anger it can be really hard to pause and think especially when the only thought in your head is to hurt severely the person you dislike, but for the benefit of yourself you must think with a mindful response and use this acronym as an aid (THINK).

THINK! THINK! THINK! THINK! THINK! THINK! THINK! THINK! THINK!

What am I really reacting to?

What is it really that is pushing my buttons?

What is it that I think is going to happen?

What is the worst (and best) that could happen?

What is most likely to happen?

Am I making a micro issue or a macro problem?

Am I over-reacting?

Am I getting things out of proportion?

How important will this matter be in six months from now?

What harm has actually been done?

Can I just let the matter go truly?

Have I got more important things to stress about?

Am I underestimating my ability to cope?

Am I overestimating the danger?

What advice would I give someone else in this situation?

What would be the consequences, if I react to violence?

Is it truly worth committing violence over & risking my freedom?

Do I have the option to walk away?

A wise man is he who thinks with a mindful response through asking self-analytical questions (such as those above) when forced with anger?

Combat feelings of anger as if anger itself is your enemy. Anger is a hot emotion and it is only the foolish that put their hands in fire (something hot) knowing the effects are likely to be harmful. This is the example I present of one who welcomes anger with violence. On the other hand, the wise person weighs up the options, calculates the risks and realises the consequences, then will **WALK AWAY**.

Wisest

Always

Leaves

Knowing

And

Walks

Award

Yard

The above acronym is the philosophy of a lifer prisoner named Dwayne Lock whom stated: "One day, one moment, one second of anger can cost two precious lives. One in a grave and the other rotting like me serving this life sentence. I was not wise but a wise man always leaves the violent situation knows it is not worth it and walks away yard (i.e. home). In other words what he meant was the Wisest person will Always Leave Knowing once he has calculated the consequences that violence is not worth the problems it escalates and as a result will crush their ego by stepping on it, so much so that even if they are right - for the sake of benefit they will leave And Walk Away Yard (i.e. Home)"

One must remember that the faculty to 'THINK' is a prerequisite for one to 'WALK AWAY'. A psychologist once said *"DBT (Dialectic Behaviour Therapy) course trains you to THINK before acting. It is about reasoning, repercussion before action."*

A lifer prisoner name Jeffery Lartey (i.e. once known as Bully) stated: *"You walk away from one problem and you save on a thousand".* My point I emphasise to encourage think before you act. Lifers have had a lot of time to think about their actions and unknowingly produce sound statements. So, if I was you, I would take heed before hindsight before it is too late. The wise person learns from other mistakes without having to experience it and this allows them to develop great foresight.

Whilst in prison myself, I had monthly appointments by choice with a psychologist and I undertook these sessions which helped address my thinking skills. I was encouraged to think in a pragmatic way when I was angry. I was told you must think 'APPLE'. It sounded so stupid, I laughed but it actually makes sense even as a peculiar acronym, which is even more of a reason why I remember 'APPLE'.

Now, every time I get angry my natural response is to think of **'APPLE'** and my anger fades away. 'APPLE' is an acronym, which stands for;

Acknowledge

Pause

Pull back

Let go

Explore

(Copyright: https://www.getselfhelp.co.uk/apple.htm)

I read it to myself every morning and it has helped me a lot. I stuck the poster on the wall next to my prison bed until it became inculcated. In fact, the two acronyms 'THINK' and 'WALK AWAY' were derived from lifer prisoners. Both prisoners Jeffery Lartey and Dwayne Lock strongly shaped the solutions in this chapter due to their creative input and life experience.

Myself, I am a brand-new person and cannot remember the old me as he was buried many years ago. I have had nine years and counting of prison time to THINK or as I like to call it 'me time'.

Lifers have had enough time to ruminate, reflect and THINK about life, which allows them to investigate religion for solace, hope and forgiveness. After time of exploring the matter many choose Islam as a way of life due to its highlighted truths and no one can deny truth except for those who are ignorant. Myself also being Muslim when researching Islamic views on anger was surprised to find the practical and useful religious solutions.

RELIGIOUS SOLUTIONS

I am a Muslim and follow the religion of Islam, which has helped me in many aspects of my life whether it be morally, financially, emotionally or ethics in other fields. More importantly pertinent to the subject at hand - I have learnt practical religious solutions, which have helped me a lot and here they are for you too, as you may possibly benefit.

In this chapter it provides practical assistance to the cause of violence (i.e. anger). Because anger is a catalyst for one who acts violently. It was only in prison where I had unwanted time to reflect on my personality, study myself and rectify my actions and character or any other issues I had, according to the beautiful religion of Islam when you study its history.

The prophet Muhammed (pbuh) has the largest population of following worldwide to be known as the last prophet to be sent by god (Allah) - to be a seal of prophecy. He had very wise words which were documented (i.e. hadiths) and remain till today even after 1400 years since his death.

I have painstakingly researched and referred as much as I could about what the Prophet Muhammad (pbuh) stated regarding anger. Please do bear in mind; I was confined to a prison cell at the time of writing this book. Therefore, I had limited access to facilities, books plus no internet meaning I only have tethered access to reading material from the prison library.

I will now introduce hadiths regarding anger narrated by the Prophet Muhammad (pbuh):

A judge should not make a judgment between two persons when he is in anger (Page 1025, summarised Sahih al-Bukhari by Dr Muhammad Muhsin Khan)

The above hadith clearly epitomizes that there is no doubt that anger distorts sound judgement because judgement is the faculty of reasoning. Therefore, anger does allow one to think straight and use their own logic appropriately.

The powerful one is not he who overpowers somebody to the ground, but the powerful one is he who restrains himself whilst angry
(Sahih al-Bukhari)

Every human has had a bitter taste of anger and will understand through an experience the extreme difficulty to refrain by not reacting with violence. Therefore, reacting with violence is the easy option but true power is the ability to control one's self in such a dissolute state of anger.

Teach and makes things easy, do not make them difficult, if anyone of you becomes angry let him keep silent
(Sahih al Bukhari)

The solution in the previous hadith mentioned is the perks of silence and I have already listed many benefits of silence in an earlier chapter on page 29.

"Anger is an ember of fire" (Sahih al Bukhari)

If it states anger is an ember of fire, then the appropriate solution would be for one to keep cool through ablution for water extinguishes fire, this is an Islamic remedy.

Dr Muhammad Ali Hashim, Author of "The Ideal Muslim' spoke about the same epidemic of anger and wrote:

"Self-control at the time of anger is the measure of a man's manhood and discipline, because if a man can control himself at such a time; then he will be to take change of any situation, preventing conflict and trouble"

You must remember power is not necessarily always strength, but power can also be knowledge. For example, the one who is angry may think and use the faculty of reason which allows them to ruminate on the correct decision; thereby allowing the right cause of action to take place. Hence, they have complete power plus control of the situation.

Dr Aid al-Qarni, Author of 'Don't be sad', also elucidates practical advice on anger in the same book on page 230, with a specific title 'Don't be angry'. It is written the Prophet (pbuh) advised one of his companions 'Don't be angry'. He repeated this phrase three times. The chapter continues and ***Dr Aid al-Qarni states: "Anger is one of the factors that cause depression and sadness".***

The following are some of the ways of controlling your anger.

[And those who repress anger, and who pardon men; verily God loves the good-doers, Quran, 3:134]

- *Make ablution. Since anger is an ember of the fire, it can be extinguished by water*
- *If you are standing sit, if you are sitting, lie down.*
- *When you are angry, remain silent.*
- *Remind yourself of the rewards of those who repress their anger and those who forgive*

JOSHUA'S STORY

Joshua White aka Abdul Aziz was also my close friend, he meant so much to me like he was almost my twin brother. Initially, I met Joshua through a friend that I met in prison. This friend of mine does not wish to disclose his name, but we were locked up next door to each other in HMP Highpoint. We became good friends and when I was released in 2015; he gave me Joshua's number to stay in touch with him. The world is a strange place and Allah (god) works in mysterious ways; here is why.

When I first contacted Joshua I had explained how I got his number, we got to talking and then I became closer to him than the friend who introduced us whilst in prison. I realised he was the exact same copy as me and we both lived identical lives but just had different names. He was my brother from another mother you could say. In fact, we both grew up in east London, he was from Hackney and I was from Leyton. Only one road 'Lea Bridge Road' separated us but unfortunately it burns me inside even with writing this in 2019 we were completely separated as he lost his precious life to the infection of knife crime.

Joshua was exactly like me. I remember very clearly the first few conversations we had and I thought to myself *'this is crazy this guy is exactly like me'*, Some people even said that I reminded them of Joshua or vice versa. We basically knew the exact same people and shared similar outlooks on life.

My mental state and growth were exactly simultaneous or parallel to Joshua's, if not identical. We both grew up in rough areas of East London as youth, adopting one-dimensional beliefs that 'crime pays' and as a result went to prison, but upon release realised crime does not pay. In life, you live and learn through trial and error gaining hindsight leading to better foresight.

I came back to prison due to my crass mistakes and Joshua helped me a lot; he sent me twenty self help books and would continuously ask me if I needed anything to which I would say - no, you have helped me enough. People would say he was a bookworm just like me. He must be in a better place - I don't believe for even half a second that God (Allah) would let a life be lost or taken and there is no part two or second chapter to life. There must be a hereafter, where true justice and recompensation takes place. I have always said, sometimes in life you meet the best of people (i.e. Joshua) in the worst of places (i.e. Prison). He was exactly like me; we cared about our families just like everyone else but we both learned about ourselves that we had a similar young ripe crippled mentality of *'looking for the right way to do the wrong things'*, meaning trying to make crime pay so we could live a better life. We had loads of discussion about this twisted concept and we encouraged each other to change our lives around for the better.

I remember once he messaged me out of the blue one day saying 'he had enough' and I told him 'me too'. I said to him 'the street life is a disease like cancer, which will slowly kill you, so leave it before it's too late; and he did exactly that but I strongly believe *"God (Allah) plans, and we plan but God (Allah) is the best of all planners" (3:54)*.

Joshua was undertaking a PTS course to qualify for a job role in the rail industry and he had intentions to get married but never did because God (Allah) has something better planned for him. We sometimes cannot comprehend why God does what he wills and the way life functions mysteriously because this is exactly what Joshua would have said had the roles have been reversed and I was lying six feet under. My religious shaped beliefs are that behind every struggle, pain or challenge in life there is unknown wisdom foreign to human kind, and only known to God (Allah). We have very little of life figured out.

What really frustrates me more than anything is that Joshua was not a murderer; he never shot or stabbed anyone. So, no-one on this earth has the right to murder him. I know I have done bad things in my life and have been responsible for some criminal activity but I pleaded guilty and nobody lost their life.

In my life now in hindsight, I am seriously against knife and gun crime. It really causes more problems than it solves. These youth that are going around stabbing each other are not really murderers they react under pressure, then brag on you tube through music about stabbings and shootings. It is pathetic as well as laughable due to its foolishness. I have been convicted of possession of a bladed article and served a prison sentence for it. It held the same crass thought process that: "I have to have a knife for self-protection, they may have a knife and they are going to kill me". This is the way a coward would think because they are afraid of death and attempting to avoid the inevitable. I realised from prison-thinking that we are both the problem and solution; no matter how hard you try we cannot escape death whether you carry one knife or two guns - it does not matter it is unavailable, death is something we must all accept. In fact, if you really want to reduce the chances of death, then how about quitting that street life and changing your perspective.

What opened my eye and made me realise that including myself and all these youth that carry knives and guns - it is nothing but pretence of pressure, because you are not ready for the consequences of a murderer (i.e. life sentence or death due to revenge). Truly it is not in you to be a murderer, killer or that guy 'catching a body'. It does not make any logical sense; you want to kill someone but are not prepared for the life sentence or death itself. You want to put your hand in fire but not get burnt and this is the only example I could possibly think of to describe such a delusional scenario.

It is definitely not for me, you or anyone else to take another humans life. Life is not a joke and it is very precious; it is not a game where you can get killed and respawn. There really is no coming back once you are gone, you are gone for real.

It is getting ridiculous; someone somewhere has to put that knife down or that gun away. When will it stop?

I am the same kid from the streets who has been convicted for possession of ammunition and a bladed article, and attempted murder. Now, I am strongly against violence - killing someone is not cool and it does not make you a big man. A real big man is one who looks after others and supports those whom he loves.

Even if you lost a person you love, it does not give you the excuse to have an outrage of murder. Religion changed my life and mentality, so did it with Joshua. I'm extremely sad and will never be the same again but I'm just glad to know his last actions were that he left Friday Muslim prayers (Jummah), and departed to a better place. I would really like to ask those responsible, what was the need and why? Because he was not out to kill anyone. If anyone thinks violence is the answer then they have a lot of mental growth to yet succeed, because violence is not cool.

Joshua wasn't only killed but the atmosphere in his mother's house has been killed too. His presence and company have been killed too. No mother deserves the pain for the loss of her son.

Even the way I feel when I heard of his death was a shock to me and I seriously cannot comprehend his mother's pain, the youth of today are ruining their own life as well as so many other people. I have lived the sadistic 'street life' to tell the story and I am the same person once had a crippled mentality of 'IDGAF' but now have a completely different outlook on life. I was that kid who could not care less if someone died as long as it was not me or anyone that I loved, but my perspective and mind frame has completely changed.

The way I felt when I lost Joshua is a feeling I would not wish on any single human. I cried yeah; I felt to puke yeah because of the fact that he was stabbed in the heart and my mind was unsettled. I felt dizzy, sickened and upset plus some of it I can't describe and at the same time I felt numb or emotionless. I just have to understand he is not coming back again and all I can do is hope through prayer that we meet again in heaven (god willing).

Violence is not cool, because prison is mental torture and the grave - well there is no experience for such a circumstance. It just makes me sick and I am tired of hearing all these stabbings in the country, especially in London with people dying. Life is already hard just the way it is, so why make it anymore harder or difficult for yourself and everyone else innocent along the journey. I'm the same kid who was just like you, that did not care about any life until I actually lost a loved one. My whole life has changed and it will never be the same. I'm just saying there are so many other ways to solve a problem rather than stabbing someone to kill them. There is no void reason for taking someone's life, because life is precious and anything that is precious must be cherished with care. Just remember, before you think to pick up that knife or gun - you could be next to die or end up rotting in a prison cell year after year for life.

CONCLUSION

This book I have written within a confined prison cell is nothing but on attempt to share my crazy experience with you from prison and the ugly 'street life'. It is for you to share with others you may know it applies to even though it may not apply to you. Maybe you have a young family member on the wrong path who may value or act upon some of the beneficial knowledge in this book. That is the strongest reason why I even wrote this. I did not have the opportunity to do so or even learn how to combat anger and violence until I came prison. It has been a very long learning curve in my life with its drastic twists due to my foolish decision-making at a young age.

Anger is a universal problem in every culture; it is a human fabric which is venomous to communities. You have to THINK and WALK AWAY to dissect anger for the better of yourself. Otherwise, there is a possibility that you will THINK whilst in handcuffs as you WALK AWAY from freedom to prison. Anger is deceptive for it is nothing but a provocation - it is just a response to a situation or someone. Anger is a negative magnet that attracts more badness. Anger is an emotion no human can avoid but can control. Anger is the grandson of conflict and violence is the father of anger but they all are related through a grievous matter. Anger brings no good as you touch the lives of others in a negative manner and self-inflict unwanted problems in your own life. Anger is toxic, poison and venomous.

The only way anger can be good is if you channel it into motivation for a positive aim (i.e. take up boxing as a vocation to vent your anger and try even go professional). There are loads of ways to transform a negative into a positive. (Book recommendation: How To Turn Negativity Into Positivity by Adzz The Author)

Violence is never the answer to anger, but when is it okay to use violence? Well, according to the UK law - self protection with responsible force is the only occasion but even then you should try your best to avoid conflict at all costs because one punch, one knife, one bullet can change two lives or even more in a detrimental way. One spur of the moment decision is not worth the life-long consequences effecting you and others around you.

Violence is not cool; take the words of hindsight from a prisoner who has spent years and years reflecting due to a violent act a young age with a stupid mind-set. My advice 'cure violence with silence' - because silence allows you to THINK clearly and come to the decision of being smart as you WALK AWAY from one problem to solve a thousand.

My message

THINK and WALK AWAY.